W9-BGZ-939

FREAKY FISH

Pufferfish

BY THERESE M. SHEA

Gareth Stevens
PUBLISHING

Please visit our website, www.garethstevens.com. For a free color catalog of all our high-quality books, call toll free 1-800-542-2595 or fax 1-877-542-2596.

Library of Congress Cataloging-in-Publication Data

Names: Shea, Therese, author.
Title: Pufferfish / Therese M. Shea.
Description: New York : Gareth Stevens Publishing, [2018] | Series: Freaky fish | Includes index.
Identifiers: LCCN 2017008902| ISBN 9781538202678 (pbk. book) | ISBN 9781538202494 (6 pack) | ISBN 9781538202609 (library bound book)
Subjects: LCSH: Puffers (Fish)–Juvenile literature.
Classification: LCC QL638.T32 S54 2018 | DDC 597/.64–dc23
LC record available at https://lccn.loc.gov/2017008902

First Edition

Published in 2018 by
Gareth Stevens Publishing
111 East 14th Street, Suite 349
New York, NY 10003

Copyright © 2018 Gareth Stevens Publishing

Designer: Katelyn E. Reynolds
Editor: Joan Stoltman

Photo credits: Cover, p. 1 Beth Swanson/Shutterstock.com; cover, pp. 1–24 (background) Ensuper/Shutterstock.com; cover, pp. 1–24 (background) macro-vectors/Shutterstock.com; cover, pp. 1–24 (background) Kjpargeter/Shutterstock.com; cover, pp. 1–24 (fact box)nicemonkey/Shutterstock.com; p. 4 NPS photo - Bryan Harry/Bricktop/Wikipedia.org; p. 5 Dave Fleetham/Design Pics/Perspectives/Getty Images; p. 7 ekler/Shutterstock.com; p. 9 (inset) Jung Hsuan/Shutterstock.com; p. 9 (main) T. Ozair/Shutterstock.com; p. 11 (inset) fenkieandreas/Shutterstock.com; p. 11 (main) Jeff Rotman/Photolibrary/Getty Images; p. 13 ReinhardDirscherl/ullstein bild via Getty Images; p. 15 Jeff Rotman/Oxford Scientific/Getty Images; p. 16 Richard Whitcombe/Shutterstock.com; p. 17 The Asahi Shimbun via Getty Images; p. 19 YOSHIKAZU TSUNO/AFP/Getty Images; p. 21 Isabelle Kuehn/Shutterstock.com.

Printed in the United States of America

CPSIA compliance information: Batch #CS17GS: For further information contact Gareth Stevens, New York, New York at 1-800-542-2595.

CONTENTS

Words in the glossary appear in **bold** type the first time they are used in the text.

A Swell Fish

Imagine catching a fish, and then—only a few seconds later—it swells up like a balloon! The pufferfish does just that, but it doesn't do it for fun. Swelling up makes it too big to swallow, **protecting** it from getting eaten by predators.

This cool trick isn't the only **adaptation** the pufferfish has to keep itself safe. It's also very, very poisonous. Also called the puffer or blowfish, these are truly freaky—and sometimes frightening—fish!

The pufferfish expands, or puffs, when it feels it's in danger.

5

The Pufferfish Population

There are more than 120 species, or kinds, of pufferfish around the world living in all sorts of warm **habitats.** Most live in the oceans, but some live in freshwater. Others like brackish water, which is a mix of freshwater and salt water.

Pufferfish can be really small or very large. The dwarf, or pygmy, puffer is 1 inch (2.5 cm) long. The giant puffer can grow to be more than 2 feet (61 cm) long. That's a big difference!

FREAKY FACT!

The dwarf pufferfish can only be found in one river in India!

WHERE ARE PUFFERFISH FOUND?

Pufferfish aren't usually found in the coldest waters on Earth, but they're found nearly everywhere else!

NORTH AMERICA

EUROPE

ASIA

Atlantic Ocean

AFRICA

Pacific Ocean

Pacific Ocean

SOUTH AMERICA

Indian Ocean

AUSTRALIA

ANTARCTICA

pufferfish range

FREAKY FORMS

Pufferfish are certainly freaky when they blow up, but their normal shape is strange, too! They're usually short with a fat head, small fins, and big eyes. They have four teeth that **fuse** together to make a kind of beak. It's used to break open shells when eating animals like crabs and snails.

Pufferfish have rough, tough skin that's often patterned. Some species have spines, or spikes, on their skin. These lay flat against the body until a fish puffs up.

FREAKY FACT!
Fishermen usually use gloves when handling pufferfish because they don't want to touch their painful spikes!

Most predators know to stay away from something with spines. Those who don't will learn that lesson quickly enough. Ouch!

BLOWING UP

Scientists think the pufferfish **developed** these freaky adaptations over time because they're such bad swimmers.

Faster ocean creatures easily catch them, but when they do, the pufferfish starts quickly taking in water, filling up like a water balloon. Their skin even stretches until it's so tight it might burst! But it never does. The predator can't swallow a fish so big, so it lets go! Pufferfish can also do this with air when they're caught by fishermen or birds and taken out of water.

FREAKY FACT!

Some pufferfish can even change their coloring! Scientists think they do this to tell other fish they're poisonous!

Some pufferfish are brightly colored, which tells other animals that they're dangerous. Other pufferfish aren't very colorful, though.

DON'T MESS WITH THIS MONSTER

When an animal actually does manage to eat pufferfish, they're in for quite a nasty surprise. Pufferfish are one of the most poisonous creatures on Earth! The poison can come out a pufferfish's spikes or be **released** by other body parts. The poison is not only deadly, though. It also doesn't taste good. Double yuck!

A pufferfish makes enough poison in its body to kill as many as 30 people! And unlike some poisons, there's no **antidote** to stop its effects.

FREAKY FACT!
Tiger sharks and sea snakes are pufferfish predators that aren't harmed by its poison!

Hopefully, this tiny pufferfish has puffed up enough to save himself!

13

CHOWING DOWN

Many different kinds of animals are predators to pufferfish, but pufferfish are also predators themselves! In fact, they eat many different kinds of animals. Some pufferfish eat **algae** and plankton, which include different kinds of tiny plants and animals that live and float in water.

Larger pufferfish eat worms, shrimp, lobsters, sea stars, crabs, and clams. Their four sharp teeth can break through an animal's outer shell to get at the soft body within. Yum!

FREAKY FACT!

Pufferfish teeth keep growing their whole life. Eating hard things wears their teeth down. If their teeth get too long, they can't close their mouth to eat!

Even though they only have
four teeth, pufferfish do just
fine eating most shelled sea creatures!

FISH FRY

Pufferfish have a freaky **life cycle.** A male pufferfish pushes the female to shore so that she can lay eggs. The eggs float on the water for about a week and then **hatch.** A baby pufferfish, called a fry, keeps its eggshell until its tail, fins, and other body parts are finished growing a few days later.

Now that the fry has fins and a tail, it finds a home. Pufferfish usually live 4 to 8 years!

young ring pufferfish

Laying eggs isn't always a peaceful event for pufferfish. Check out these grass pufferfish **spawning** on the shores of Japan!

DEADLIEST DISH

Some people eat these poisonous fish! Pufferfish are used in a Japanese dish called fugu. It takes more than a year to learn how to cook this fish in a way that makes it safe. Even still, about five people a year die from eating it!

Scientists found out that pufferfish make their poison from bacteria they collect while they eat. Knowing that, some people raise pufferfish in bacteria-free habitats so that they can grow without a chance of developing poison.

FREAKY FACT!

When a person's been poisoned by a pufferfish, at first they can't feel their mouth. Then, as the poison moves through the body, it shuts down different body systems until death occurs. Yikes!

Chefs must learn to carefully remove the poisonous parts of the pufferfish before serving fugu.

19

FANTASTIC FISH

Pufferfish can be kept as pets! The ones in pet shops aren't poisonous because they weren't raised in the wild. You'll need to feed them food like shrimp, worms, and plenty of shellfish to keep their teeth short. Or leave the pufferfish care to your local aquarium, and check them out when you visit!

Scientists are still discovering new species of pufferfish. One kind even creates beautiful patterns in the sand on the seafloor to draw in partners! There's still so much to learn about pufferfish!

FREAKY FACT!

In a tank, pufferfish need to be kept away from other fish so they don't eat the fish!

Pufferfish can be cute, but don't get close!

GLOSSARY

adaptation: a change in a type of animal that makes it better able to live in its surroundings

algae: living plantlike things that are mostly found in water

antidote: something that stops the harmful effects of a poison

develop: to grow, create, or change over time

fuse: to join or combine (different things) together

habitat: the natural place where an animal or plant lives

hatch: to break open or come out of

life cycle: the stages through which a living thing passes from the beginning of its life until its death

protect: to keep safe

release: to let free

spawning: when animals (such as fish or frogs) go to lay eggs

FOR MORE INFORMATION

BOOKS

Markovics, Joyce. *Puffer Fish*. New York, New York: Bearport Publishing, 2016.

Rudenko, Dennis. *Look Out for the Pufferfish!* New York, NY: PowerKids Press, 2016.

Schuh, Mari. *Pufferfish*. Minneapolis, MN: Bullfrog Books, 2016.

WEBSITES

Crop Circles of the Sea: Product of the Pufferfish
kidsdiscover.com/quick-reads/crop-circles-sea-product-pufferfish/
Read this great article about how and why pufferfish make patterns on the ocean floor!

Puffer Fish
a-z-animals.com/animals/puffer-fish/
Read much more about these amazing fish.

Pufferfish
animals.nationalgeographic.com/animals/fish/pufferfish/
Check out some colorful photos of pufferfish.

INDEX